TABLE OF CONTENTS

HEROINE STORIES

What does heroine mean?
What types of roles do women play in most folktales?
What types of roles should women play in folktales?

Heroes are brave people. They're main characters in stories. **Heroines** are female heroes.

There are more male heroes than heroines in stories. In most folktales, women have weak roles. They wait to be saved by men. Or they help male heroes. In some stories, women are **wicked**. Wicked means evil or bad. Women may play **villains**. Villains are the criminals. They fight against heroes.

• •

"Damsel in distress" is a common role for women. Damsel means girl. Distress means in trouble.

STONE CIRCLE STORIES:
CULTURE AND FOLKTALES

HEROINE STORIES

BY VIRGINIA LOH-HAGAN

People have been telling stories since the beginning of time. This series focuses on stories found across cultures. You may have heard these stories from your parents or grandparents. Or you may have told one yourself around a campfire. Stories explain the world around us. They inspire. They motivate. They even scare! We tell stories to share our history.

45th Parallel Press

Published in the United States of America by Cherry Lake Publishing
Ann Arbor, Michigan
www.cherrylakepublishing.com

Reading Adviser: Marla Conn MS, Ed., Literacy specialist, Read-Ability, Inc.
Book Designer: Jen Wahi

Photo Credits: ©Phil Jones/Shutterstock.com, 5; ©Alexander Lukatskiy/Shutterstock.com, 7; ©spatuletail/Shutterstock.
com, 8; ©chippix/Shutterstock.com, 11; ©Anne Power/Shutterstock.com, 13; ©jaimie tuchman/Shutterstock.com, 14;
©SSokolov/Shutterstock.com, 17; ©Harris Channing/Shutterstock.com, 19; ©B Christopher/Shutterstock.com, 21;
©Oleg Golovnev/Shutterstock.com, 23; ©Sogno Lucido/Shutterstock.com, 25; ©Rakkandee/Shutterstock.com, 27;
©Richard A McMillin/Shutterstock.com, 28; ©aleg baranau/Shutterstock.com, cover and interior; Various grunge/
texture patterns throughout courtesy of Shutterstock.com

45th Parallel Press is an imprint of Cherry Lake Publishing.

Library of Congress Cataloging-in-Publication Data

Names: Loh-Hagan, Virginia, author.
Title: Heroine stories / by Virginia Loh-Hagan.
Description: [Ann Arbor : Cherry Lake Publishing, 2019] | Series: Stone
   circle stories: Culture and folktales | Includes bibliographical references and index.
Identifiers: LCCN 2018035178| ISBN 9781534143517 (hardcover) | ISBN
   9781534140073 (pbk.) | ISBN 9781534141278 (pdf) | ISBN 9781534142473
   (hosted ebook)
Subjects: | CYAC: Heroes--Folklore. | Folklore.
Classification: LCC PZ8.1.L936 Her 2019 | DDC [398.2]--dc23
LC record available at https://lccn.loc.gov/2018035178

Printed in the United States of America
Corporate Graphics

ABOUT THE AUTHOR:

Dr. Virginia Loh-Hagan is an author, university professor, and former classroom teacher. She dedicates this book to the heroines in her life story! She lives in San Diego with her very tall husband and very naughty dogs. To learn more about her, visit www.virginialoh. com.

They can save themselves. Women are just as powerful and interesting as males. Heroes come in all shapes and sizes.

CHAPTER 1

SALLY ANN THUNDER ANN WHIRLWIND CROCKETT

Who is Sally Ann Thunder Ann Whirlwind Crockett?
Why is she special?
Who is Davy Crockett?

Tall tales are special stories. They're told as if they're true. But they're not. Sally Ann Thunder Ann Whirlwind Crockett is a tall tale heroine.

Sally Ann came from a family of nine boys. Her brothers didn't want anything to do with a girl.

This story is from Tennessee.

Sally Ann said, "Brothers, let me tell you something.
Whatever you can do, I can do better!"

She was tough. She was funny. She was sweet. She was
pretty. She said, "I'm off to seek adventure." She slept
with bears. She ran with wolves. She swam with sharks.

One day, Sally Ann found a man stuck in a tree. That man was Davy Crockett. Sally Ann saw a nest of snakes. She tied the snakes together. She made a rope. She threw the rope at a branch. She tugged. She set Crockett free.

Sally Ann and Crockett fell in love. They got married. They had 10 kids. They were happy.

Crockett was proud of Sally Ann. He **bragged** about her skills. Brag means to show off. He said, "She wrestles alligators until they beg for their life."

Davy Crockett was a real person. He was an American cowboy and politician.

SPOTLIGHT BIOGRAPHY

Elizabeth Holloway Marston was an inspiration for Wonder Woman. Wonder Woman is the first mainstream female superhero. She's a warrior with special powers. She was created in 1941. She was created by Marston's husband, William Moulton Marston William wanted to create a special superhero who would be the new Superman. Marston told her husband that the superhero should be a woman. Marston lived from 1893 to 1993. She was born in Boston. She died a month after her 100th birthday. She was a lawyer and psychologist. She was one of the first women to graduate from law school. She helped create a lie detector test. This is a machine that measures blood pressure. People get nervous when they lie. This machine inspired the Lasso of Truth. Lasso means rope. It's one of Wonder Woman's weapons.

Mike Fink was a boat captain. He didn't like Crockett's bragging. He said, "I bet I can scare Sally Ann. I'll scare hcr so badly her teeth will fall out. If I lose, I'll give you a dozen wildcats."

Crockett took the bet. He said, "You'll never trick my wife. She's too smart for you."

Fink took the skin of an alligator. He wrapped it around himself. He hid in the bushes. When Sally Ann came by, he jumped out. He roared. Sally Ann wasn't fooled. She just laughed.

Fink got mad. He came toward her. Sally Ann didn't like this. She said, "Don't come near me." Fink didn't listen. Sally Ann took out her toothpick. She hit the alligator's head. The head, along with Fink's hair, flew into the sky.

Sally Ann told her husband what happened. Crockett laughed. He said, "You're the toughest lady in the West. No one will bother you again."

Sally Ann Thunder Ann Whirlwind Crockett wasn't a real person.

CHAPTER 2

BIG LIZ

Who is Big Liz?
Why did the master want to kill her?
How did she get even with the master?

Big Liz is a character from African American folktales. She was a **slave**. Slaves were stolen from Africa. They were forced to work on plantations. Plantations are big farms. They were owned by **masters**. The masters were rich white men.

Big Liz was big. She was tall. She was strong. She could pick up two big pigs. She carried them like they were air. She won every fight.

Many historic plantations are found in the South.

The U.S. Civil War was fought between the Northern and Southern states. The North didn't want slavery. The South wanted slavery. Big Liz's master wanted the South to win. He sent food and money. But Big Liz told Northern soldiers about it. She was a spy. She risked her life. She was brave.

The swamp is in Maryland. It's called the Greenbriar Swamp.

The master found out. He was mad. He knew he couldn't fight Big Liz. So he tried to trick her. He gave her the heaviest box of gold. He said, "Big Liz, can you help me? Here's a box of gold. I need to get it to the Southern army. Bury it so the Northern army can't find it."

Big Liz carried the heavy box to a swamp. The master was secretly following her. She dug a deep hole. She got stuck. The master confronted her. Confront means to

FAST-FORWARD TO MODERN TIMES

Feminism supports equality between men and women. It supports women's rights and interests. Today, there are more feminist folktales. These are stories that feature women heroines. Women get trapped. They get in danger. But they don't wait for men to save them. They save themselves. They save others. They fight villains. They escape. They're independent. They're smart. They're strong. They're fearless. They live freely. They live happily. In some stories, there are role reversals. Reversal means switching. This means that women act like men and men act like women. An example is when the man takes care of children. And the woman makes money. In other feminist folktales, writers rewrite popular stories. They change details to make women the heroes. They don't have princesses waiting to be saved by Prince Charming. They have princesses taking charge.

face in challenge. He said, "You're a spy! There's only one way to deal with a spy." He took out a sword. He chopped off her head. Her head rolled away from the hole. But her body stayed in the hole. The master filled in the hole. He didn't look for Big Liz's head. It was too dark.

The master walked home. He felt someone watching him. He heard footsteps behind him. He got scared. He ran. He saw the lights of his house. He was almost home. Then, Big Liz's ghost got in his path. She was holding her head. She put it down. She grabbed the master's neck. Big Liz killed him. She left his body to rot. She picked up her head. She went back to the swamp.

Today, people drive to the swamp. They go at midnight. They honk three times. They flash their car lights two times. Big Liz comes out. She watches the gold. She won't let the Southern army get it.

People say they can see Big Liz's red glowing eyes.

CHAPTER 3

ANNIE CHRISTMAS

Who is Annie Christmas?

How is she a heroine?

What happened between her and Mike Fink?

Annie Christmas was an African American woman. She was a **keelboat** captain. Keelboats are pulled by poles. It takes a lot of power to pull these boats. Christmas was super strong. She could lift anything. She worked harder than 10 men. The ground shook when she yelled. She wasn't married. She had 12 sons. All her sons worked on her boat. Her boat was named *Big River's Daughter*.

Annie Christmas is also known as Keelboat Annie.

Christmas was 7 feet (2 meters) tall. She weighed 250 pounds (113 kilograms). She had a loud laugh. She had beautiful dark skin. She dressed in men's clothes during the day. At night, she wore a red silk dress. She wore a hat with feathers.

She wore a long pearl necklace. Each pearl stood for someone she **defeated**. Defeat means to beat or to win

CROSS-CULTURAL CONNECTION

Li Chi is a heroine. She appears in Chinese folktales. There's an evil snake. This snake killed people in Li Chi's town. The town had to give it a 13-year-old girl every year. The snake would eat this girl. This was the only way to save the town. The town did this for 9 years. One year, Li Chi volunteered. Li Chi's family had six girls and no boys. Li Chi went to the snake's cave. She brought a sword, dog, and rice balls. She put the rice balls in front of the cave. Then, she hid. The snake ate the rice balls. Li Chi's dog attacked the snake. Li Chi jumped on the snake's back. She stabbed her sword into the snake. The snake died. Li Chi found the bones of the other girls. She said, "You were weak girls. That's why the snake ate you. I'm strong." She went back to her town. She became the queen.

over. She beat up bullies. She took on dares and won. When she died, her necklace was over 30 feet (9 m) long.

There was a boat. It wasn't Christmas' boat. The boat got trapped in a storm. Christmas told the captain to turn around. The captain didn't listen to her. The boat was sinking. Christmas took charge. She helped people get on her boat. She jumped in the water. She tied the boat to her waist. She pulled the boat to shore. She made sure people were safe. People wanted to be "as strong as Annie Christmas."

Annie Christmas appears in tall tales from Louisiana.

Christmas got into a fight with Mike Fink. Fink was strong. He also was a boat captain. But he wasn't very smart. And he didn't think much of women. He saw Christmas loading her boat. He said, "You should be home making socks. You shouldn't be doing men's work."

Christmas didn't like Fink. She said, "Stop talking. You don't know anything." She lifted a big box. She threw it in the river. This caused a big wave. The wave swept Fink away. It took Fink over 150 miles (241 kilometers) away. Christmas went back to work. She never saw Fink again.

Annie Christmas is known as the "female John Henry."

CHAPTER 4

SHE-WHO-LIVES-ALONE

Who is She-Who-Lives-Alone?
What did she do?
Why is she special?

The Comanche people are Native Americans. They're from the Texas area. They tell a story about She-Who-Lives-Alone.

Long ago, the ground got really dry. There was a **drought**. Droughts are times when there's little rain. Nothing grew. There was no food. There was no water. Animals and people were dying. They were **starving**. Starving means really hungry.

The Comanche people moved around a lot.

People danced. They drummed. They prayed for rain. Leaders went to search for answers. They climbed a high hill. They asked the Great Spirit for help. The Great Spirit is like a god.

The leaders returned to town. They said, "We're being punished. We've been too selfish. We need to give a **sacrifice**." They had to give up something special to get something.

She-Who-Lives-Alone was a little girl. Her family starved to death. She lived alone. She was an **orphan**. Orphans are children whose parents died.

She-Who-Lives-Alone heard the leaders. She went home. She thought about how she could help. She loved her doll. She slept with it every night. The doll was made by her grandmother. It was made from buffalo skin. Its face was painted with blueberry juice. Its hair was a blue jay's feathers.

She-Who-Lives-Alone went to the fire. She kissed her doll. She threw it in the fire. She said, "Great Spirit, this is the most valuable thing I have. It's all I have left of my family. Take her. Send rain to my people."

She waited for the fire to die down. She scooped the ashes. She threw them in the wind. She went to bed. When she woke up, there was rain. A few days later,

Comanche people lived in tipis. These are cone-shaped tents.

beautiful blue flowers grew all over the hills and valleys. The flowers were bluebonnets. They were the same color as the doll's hair and skin.

The people were happy. They changed the little girl's name. They called her One-Who-Dearly-Loves-Her-People.

Bluebonnets are the official state flower of Texas.

DID YOU KNOW?

> In stories, women appear as good fairies or wicked witches. Some scientists think this is because of how children see their mothers. Mothers can be seen as two people. Mothers can be mean. They make children follow rules. They punish children. Mothers can also be nice. They feed children. They care for them. They protect them.

> Baba Yaga is a popular female character. She's from Russian folktales. Baba Yaga is bony. She has a hooked nose. She has long, iron teeth. She kidnaps children. She eats them.

> There are more female superheroes. Jean Grey is popular. She's part of the X-Men. She's as powerful as the top male characters. She can make anything disappear. She can move objects with her mind. She can control people's minds. She's saved the world many times!

> Wonder Woman never wore a skirt. This is because it's hard to fight in skirts.

CHALLENGE:

WRITE YOUR OWN TALE

BEFORE YOU WRITE:

❯ Read more folktales with heroines. Use them as models. Learn from them.

❯ Make a list of your favorite folktales or fairy tales. Fairy tales are stories with magic. Choose one of the stories. Imagine what it would be like if the hero was a female. Think how the story would be different. Think how the details would be changed.

❯ Think about a female heroine. Make a list of her traits. Make a list of her strengths. Make a list of her weaknesses.

AS YOU WRITE:

❯ Create a setting. Describe when the story takes place. Describe where the story takes place.

❯ Describe the heroine's goal. Put someone or something in danger. Have the heroine save the day.

❯ Describe the heroine's adventure. Create trouble for your heroine. Show how the heroine overcame the dangers. Show what the heroine achieved.

❯ Describe the heroine's reward or lesson.

AFTER YOU WRITE:

❯ Proofread and edit the story.

❯ Add details to make the story more interesting.

❯ Share the story with others. Ask others for feedback. Ask others for ways to improve the story.

❯ Create a collection of stories with heroines. Use the same heroine. Write different adventures for the heroine. Or write different stories with different heroines.

CONSIDER THIS!

TAKE A POSITION! Are men and women treated equally in real life? Are they treated equally in stories? Why or why not? Argue your point with reasons and evidence.

SAY WHAT? Learn more about the folktales about Davy Crockett. Reread the chapter about Sally Ann Thunder Ann Whirlwind Crockett. Compare them. Explain how they're the same. Explain how they're different. (Remember that Davy Crockett was a real person. Not all the stories about him were true, though. Sally Ann Thunder Ann Whirlwind Crockett was not a real person.)

THINK ABOUT IT! Make a list of the heroines in your life. Who are they? How did they help you? How did they inspire you? Write thank-you notes to them.

> Girls rule the world in these stories.

LEARN MORE!

Don, Lari. *Girls and Goddesses: Stories of Heroines from Around the World*. Minneapolis: Darby Creek, 2016.

Johnston Phelps, Ethel (ed.) *Sea Girl: Feminist Folktales from Around the World*. New York: Feminist Press at CUNY, 2017.

Ragan, Kathleen (ed.) *Fearless Girls, Wise Women & Beloved Sisters: Heroines in Folktales from Around the World*. New York: W. W. Norton & Company, 2015.

Yolen, Jane. *Not One Damsel in Distress: Heroic Girls from World Folklore*. Boston: Houghton Mifflin Harcourt, 2018.

GLOSSARY

bragged (BRAGD) showed off

defeated (dih-FEET-id) beat or won over

drought (DROUT) a dry season in which there is no rain, food, or water

heroines (HER-oh-inz) female heroes, the main characters of stories

keelboat (KEEL-boht) a type of riverboat that is pulled by a pole

masters (MAS-turz) a term used to describe people who owned slaves

orphan (OR-fuhn) a child who has no living parents

sacrifice (SAK-ruh-fise) to give up something to get something in return

slave (SLAYV) a person sold to another person and forced to work

starving (STAHR-ving) being really hungry

tall tales (TAL TAYLZ) stories that have both true and exaggerated details

villains (VIL-uhnz) characters in stories who are defeated by the heroes or heroines

wicked (WIK-id) evil

INDEX